Soliloquies of Lyd

Lydia Brown

BookLeaf Publishing

Presentation by *BookLeaf Publishing*

Web: www.bookleafpub.com

E-mail: info@bookleafpub.com

ISBN: 9789357210980

First edition 2022

DEDICATION

Written for the happiness of the best mother in
the world, Julie Brown

PREFACE

Written in a stressful time, conjuring all the thoughts other than work.

Puzzled

Sudoku pages
Makes you feel confident, smart
..But that square was wrong

Citrus Swig

Lemonade? Limeade?
Where has all the sweetness gone
in mass-made acid punch?

Fallout

3

Animosity
Between silence, where both
know which one did wrong

Kitkat

4

Ruby chocolate time,
Influencer cocoa bean
dazzled in glitter

Seasons

Aching wintertime
A dearest, warm autumn leaves
at the soonest chance

Health Scare

Vaccine booster shot
A little prick, no quibble
You'd think, anyway

Nuclear

War and in pieces
Can you hope for the best,
When there's never change?

Pruning

Bonsai? Oh, lush but
the near harshest learning curve.
Perpetual stress

Antarctic

Penguin, winter king
Designed to thrive in nothing
Adapted to null

Furry friends

Puppy feet, tiny
Peets of happiness down hall
Endless squeaks of joy

Teatime

Biscuits in my drink
They broke, they sank, they soaked in
The last drops of caffeine

Melons

Cantaloupe madness
No question people pay wealth
Succulent goodness

Housecoat

Fluffy dressing gown
Wrapped you up in warm comfort
Cotton embraces

Manuka Tea

Milk and honey tea
Stir it 'til you feel at lull
Settling in peace

Elephants

Sometimes they forget
When it becomes too troubling
to remember more

Blinds

Venetian, turn them in
Break them in, twist the line bare
Gappy slat edges left

Ducks

Feed them bread, or wine
I don't think they would mind
Holy water birds

Embroidery

Pinch the needle thin
Thread it in, a twirl throughout
Criss-cross applesauce

CPSIA information can be obtained
at www.ICGtesting.com
Printed in the USA
BVHW051011060623
665467BV00018B/1170